Circle of Blessing

Blessings
graces
charges
doxologies

PETER DAINTY

kevin
mayhew

First published in 2005 by

KEVIN MAYHEW LTD
Buxhall, Stowmarket, Suffolk, IP14 3BW
E-mail: info@kevinmayhewltd.com

9 8 7 6 5 4 3 2 1 0

ISBN 1 84417 370 4
Catalogue No. 1500778

Cover design by Amanda Laws
Edited and typeset by Katherine Laidler

Printed and bound in Great Britain

Contents

All biblical quotations not followed by the reference RSV *(Revised Standard Version) are Peter Dainty's own translation.*

Introduction

This is a book of blessings in varied forms and for use on varied occasions. The first (and largest) section contains Blessings as they are traditionally known – asking for God's favour on people and situations. The second section contains Graces, which are blessings on meals combined with thanks for God's gifts. The third section contains Charges, which are words of challenge and encouragement, often (but not necessarily) associated with benedictions or blessings at the close of worship. The last section contains Doxologies, in which, instead of asking God to bless us, we bless God for his greatness, goodness, love and generosity, with exclamations of praise.

We as human beings, and the whole universe in which we live, are totally dependent on God for our existence. Without his blessings we could not survive. However, we are not always aware of this and like to think that we can manage very well on our own, without needing to turn to God for help, except, perhaps, in very desperate situations – like the man who cried out to God for help in his distress: 'O God, please help me. You know I've never troubled you before, and I promise that if you help me now I'll never trouble you again.' How much better to count your blessings and name them one by one, as the old song says. Try doing that if you can't sleep at night, instead of counting sheep. You should soon nod off.

Blessings like those in this book give us the opportunity to recognise our dependence on God in everyday life, as we sit at table, go out to work or lie down to sleep. They also provide us with words to use on those occasions in life when we are made especially aware of our need for God's blessing – the birth of a baby, rites of passage, seasons and festivals.

In the Old Testament, blessings (and curses) were believed to have an almost magical power, in that they actually brought about what was asked for, like self-fulfilling prophecies. I wouldn't go as far as that, because such beliefs seem to take away God's freedom and make his power subject to our whims and wishes. However, it is surely good to surround ourselves and other people, and the situations we find ourselves in, with our hopes and longings for all that is good and in tune with God's will; because by so doing we open the way for good things to happen. Jesus said, 'Ask, and you will receive, seek and you will find, knock and the door will be opened to you.' Although it is possible to interpret those words too simplistically, it is also possible to go to the other extreme and forget that prayer involves requests and expectations. We know from ordinary experience that we are more likely to receive if we ask, to find if we seek, and to have the door opened to us if we actually knock on it.

The tradition of saying grace at mealtimes combines blessing with thanksgiving, and is a simple but telling statement of our faith in the goodness of God and our dependence on him – and all in the context of familiar things. And it becomes an even stronger statement when we not only thank God for his blessings or ask him for more, but when we remember the needs of others – which brings us to the moral element in blessings.

In the New Testament, blessings continue the Old Testament tradition but with a stronger moral content. Jesus' *Beatitudes* are an obvious example of this, and the charges in Paul's letters are another. Blessings like these are not simply asking that things will go well for us and we shall be prosperous and successful, but that we should grow in grace – in the finer qualities and virtues which God wants to give us through his Holy Spirit.

That is why I have included a section of Charges in this book. Words of moral and spiritual challenge and encouragement can have a subtle influence on us when they are used in worship or at funerals, weddings or baptisms, and their words can linger and secretly enlarge our moral awareness, especially if we hear them more than once.

Finally, there is the section of Doxologies. Technically this term refers to the *Gloria in Excelsis* based on the song of the heavenly host in Luke 2:14, and to the *Gloria Patria*, the Trinitarian formula which traditionally concludes the singing of Psalms in Christian worship. In the Reformed tradition it also refers to the verse which ends three of Thomas Ken's hymns:

> Praise God, from who all blessings flow;
> praise him all creatures here below;
> praise him above, ye heavenly host;
> praise Father, Son, and Holy Ghost.

However, I have broadened its meaning to include many other acclamations of praise, biblical and non-biblical, including a medieval Jewish Doxology: Praise to the living God! translated by Max Landsberg and Newton Mann. The danger of broadening the meaning of Doxology in this way is that the main limit on what could be included is space. Therefore readers may be disappointed that something they were looking for has been left out.

So we have come full circle. First God blesses us, then we bless others, then all together we bless God with joyful songs (or shouts) of praise. The circle of blessings is never ending. Praise be to God!

PETER DAINTY

BLESSINGS

Assorted blessings

To God be glory;
to the angels honour;
to Satan confusion;
to the cross reverence;
to the church exaltation;
to the departed resurrection;
to the penitent acceptance;
to the sick and infirm recovery and healing;
to the four quarters of the world great peace
and tranquillity.
And on us who are weak and sinful
may the compassion and mercies of God
come and overshadow us continually.
Amen.

Old Syriac

May God shield me.
May God fill me.
May God keep me.
May God watch me.
May God bring me
to the land of peace,
to the country of the King,
to the peace of eternity.

Anon

We commend unto you, O Lord,
our souls and bodies,
our minds and our thoughts,
our prayers and our hopes,
our health and our work,
our life and our death,
our parents and brothers and sisters,
our benefactors and friends,
our neighbours, our countrymen,
and all Christian folk,
this day and always.

Lancelot Andrewes (1555–1626)

Bless all those who worship you,
from the rising of the sun,
to the going down of the same.
Of your goodness, give us.
With your love, inspire us.
By your Spirit, guide us.
By your power, protect us.
In your mercy, receive us;
now and always.
Amen.

Anon (Fifth century)

May the Father watch over you,
the Son, our Saviour, bless you,
and the Holy Spirit come to you –
so that you may be filled
with all the fullness of God.

Anon

God bless the field and bless the furrow,
  stream and branch and rabbit burrow,
  hill and stone and flower and tree,
  from Bristol town to Wetherby.
Bless the sun and bless the sleet,
  bless the lane and bless the street,
  bless the night and bless the day,
  from Somerset and all the way
  to the meadows of Cathay.
Bless the minnow, bless the whale,
  bless the rainbow and the hail.
Bless the nest and bless the leaf,
  bless the righteous and the thief.
Bless the wing and bless the fin,
  bless the air I travel in.
Bless the mill and bless the mouse,
  bless the miller's bricken house.
Bless the earth and bless the sea.
God bless you and God bless me.

Anon
The Robin's Song

May the right hand of the Lord
  keep us ever in old age,
  and the grace of Christ defend us from the enemy.
O Lord, direct our hearts in the way of peace,
  through Jesus Christ our Lord.
Amen.

The Book of Cerne (Ninth century)

Do thou, O God, bless unto me
 each thing mine eye doth see.
Do thou, O God, bless unto me
 each sound that reaches me.
Do thou, O God, bless unto me
 each savour that I smell.
Do thou, O God, bless unto me
 each taste my mouth doth tell;
 each sound that goes into my song,
 each ray that guides my way,
 each thing that I pursue along,
 each lure that tempts to stray;
 the zeal that seeks my living soul,
 the three that seek my heart and whole,
 do thou bless unto me.

Scottish

The Lord bless you.
May he fill your feet with dance
 and your arms with strength.
May he fill your hearts with tenderness
 and your eyes with laughter.
May he fill your ears with music
 and your nose with pleasant scents.
May he fill your mouth with jubilation
 and your heart with joy.
May he give us ever anew
 the desert graces:
 silence, fresh water and renewed hope.
May he give us all ever anew
 the strength to give hope a new face.
May the Lord bless you.
Amen.

Hermann Shaluck

Grant peace, welfare, blessing, grace,
loving kindness and mercy
to all mankind, O Lord.
Bless us, even all of us together,
with the light of your countenance,
for it is your light in dark times
which gives us blessings and mercy,
light and peace.
Give us the strength and courage
to reach out for these blessings
and to share them with our neighbour.
Blessed are you, O Lord,
who bless your people at all times
and in every hour with peace.

Jewish prayer

O God, who knowest us to be set in the midst
of so many and great dangers,
that by reason of the frailty of our nature,
we cannot always stand upright;
grant to us such strength and protection
as may support us in all dangers,
and carry us through all temptations:
through Jesus Christ our Lord.
Amen.

The Book of Common Prayer

Bless to us, O Lord,
the ground beneath our feet,
the sun above our heads,
the friends all around us,
and your image deep within us.

Anon

Lord, temper with tranquillity,
our manifold activity,
that we may do our work for thee
with very great simplicity.

Anon (Sixteenth century)

Grant us in all our duties thy help,
in all our perplexities thy guidance,
in all our dangers thy protection,
and in all our sorrows thy peace;
through Jesus Christ our Lord.

St Augustine (354–430)

O gracious and holy Father,
give us wisdom to perceive thee,
intelligence to understand thee,
diligence to seek thee,
patience to wait for thee,
a heart to meditate upon thee,
and a life to proclaim thee,
through the power of the Spirit
of Jesus Christ our Lord.

St Benedict (480–543)

God bless us every one.

A Christmas Carol

Charles Dickens (1812–1870)

Biblical blessings

And God blessed human beings
   and said to them:
Produce many children,
   fill and control the earth.
Rule over the fish in the sea,
   the birds in the air,
   and all living things that move on the earth.

Genesis 1:28

May God give you dew from heaven,
   and fruit from the earth:
   an abundance of grain and wine.
May whole peoples and nations serve you.
Rule over all your kin,
   and let them bow down to you.
Cursed be those who curse you,
   and blessed be those who bless you.

Genesis 27:28, 29
Isaac blesses Jacob, thinking that he is Esau

May the God of my Fathers bless these boys –
   the God in whose presence Abraham and Isaac lived,
   the God who has led me all my life to this very day.
May the angel who has brought me safely
   through all dangers bless them.
May my name live on through them,
   and the name of Abraham and Isaac, my fathers.
May their descendants multiply throughout the earth.

Genesis 48:15, 16
Jacob blesses his grandsons

The Lord bless you and keep you:
The Lord make his face to shine upon you,
 and be gracious to you:
The Lord lift up his countenance upon you,
 and give you peace.

Numbers 6:24-26 (RSV)
Aaron's blessing

Blessed are those who reject evil ways,
 who do not follow bad examples,
 or associate with wicked people;
 but delight in God's Law,
 and study his teaching day and night.
They shall be like trees growing by streams of water,
 bearing fruit in due season
 and leaves that do not wither.
They shall prosper in all that they do.

Psalm 1:1-3

Now go on your journey,
 with the Good Shepherd as your guide.
When you are weak and weary,
 may he give you rest and refreshment in green pastures.
When you are anxious and afraid,
 may he lead you beside still waters
 and restore your souls.
When you are confused and lost,
 may he show you the way.
When, in your busyness, you forget him,
 and wander away,
 may he come and seek you out.

When, in foolishness and selfishness,
  you are tempted to go astray,
  may he bring you back to the right path.
When you face the valley of shadows,
  may he be with you to bring you safely through.
On every step of the way put your trust in the Lord,
  your sure and loving shepherd, companion and friend,
  until he brings you home to rejoice at his table,
  and to dwell in his house for ever.
Amen.

Based on Psalm 23

May the Lord keep you from all evil.
May he keep your life.
May he keep your going out and your coming in
  from this time forth and for evermore.

Psalm 121:7, 8

Go in peace:
  the wisdom of the Wonderful Counsellor guide you,
  the strength of the Mighty God defend you,
  the love of the Everlasting Father enfold you,
  the peace of the Prince of Peace be upon you.
And the blessing of God Almighty,
  Father, Son and Holy Spirit,
  be upon you all this night and evermore.

Anon
Based on Isaiah 9:6

Blessed be the poor in spirit,
for the kingdom of heaven is already theirs.

Blessed be those who mourn,
for they shall be comforted.

Blessed be the meek,
for they shall inherit the earth.

Blessed be those who hunger and thirst for righteousness
for they shall be satisfied.

Blessed be the merciful,
for they shall receive mercy.

Blessed be the pure in heart,
for they shall see God.

Blessed be the peacemakers,
for they shall be called God's children.

Blessed be those who are persecuted in the cause
of righteousness,
for the kingdom of heaven is already theirs.

The Beatitudes: Matthew 5:3-10

Peace I leave with you;
my peace I give to you;
not as the world gives do I give to you.
Let not your hearts be troubled,
neither let them be afraid.

John 14:27 (RSV)

Blessed be those who have not seen, yet still believe.
John 20:29

May the God of hope
fill you with all joy and peace
through your believing,
so that by the power of the Holy Spirit
you may have all the hope you need.
Romans 15:13

The grace of the Lord Jesus Christ
and the love of God
and the fellowship of the Holy Spirit
be with you all.
2 Corinthians 13:14 (RSV)

Peace be to you all
with love and faith,
from God the Father
and the Lord Jesus Christ.
Grace be with all
who love our Lord Jesus Christ
with love undying.
Ephesians 6:23, 24

May God encourage your hearts,
  and bind them together in love.
May he give you the riches of full understanding,
  and the knowledge of his mystery, Jesus Christ,
  in whom are hid all the treasures
  of wisdom and knowledge;
  that, living in him,
  and being rooted and built up in him,
  you may be firm in the faith you have been taught,
  and full of thanksgiving.

Based on Colossians 2:2, 3, 6, 7

May the God of peace himself
  make you perfect in holiness,
  and keep your spirit, soul and body
  sound and blameless
  at the coming of our Lord Jesus Christ.
The faithful one who calls you
  will surely do this.

1 Thessalonians 5:23, 24

Now may our Lord Jesus Christ himself,
  and God the Father,
  who loved us and, through grace,
  gave us eternal encouragement and good hope,
  make your hearts stronger and firmer
  with every good word you speak
  and every good thing you do.

2 Thessalonians 2:16, 17

Now may the Lord of peace himself
give you peace at all times, in all ways.
The Lord be with you all.

2 Thessalonians 3:16 (RSV)

Now may the God of peace
who brought again from the dead
our Lord Jesus, the great shepherd of the sheep,
by the blood of the eternal covenant,
equip you with everything good
that you may do his will,
working in you that which is pleasing in his sight,
through Jesus Christ;
to whom be glory for ever and ever.
Amen.

Hebrews 13:20, 21 (RSV)

May the God of all grace,
who has called you
to his eternal glory in Christ,
restore, confirm and strengthen you.
To him be the dominion for ever and ever.
Amen.

1 Peter 5:10, 11 (RSV)

Grace, mercy and peace be with us,
from God the Father
and from Jesus Christ the Father's Son,
in truth and love.

2 John 3 (RSV)

Grace to you and peace,
from him who is, and who was, and who is to come,
and from the seven spirits who are before his throne,
and from Jesus Christ the faithful witness,
the first-born of the dead,
and the ruler of kings on earth.

Revelation 1:4b, 5a (RSV)

Celtic blessings

The eye of the great God be on you.
The eye of the God of glory be on you.
The eye of the Son of Mary Virgin be on you.
The eye of the Spirit mild be on you,
  to aid you and to shepherd you.
Oh the kindly eye of the Three be on you,
  to aid you and to shepherd you.

Celtic

Each day be glad to you,
  no day be sad to you,
  life rich and satisfying.

Plenty be on your course,
  a son be on your coming,
  a daughter on your arriving.

The strong help of the servant be yours,
  the strong help of the fire be yours,
  the strong help of the graces.

The love-death of joy be yours,
  the love-death of Mary be yours,
  the loving arm of your Saviour.

Celtic

I pray for you a joyous life,
honour, estate and good repute,
no sigh from your heart,
no tear from your eye.

No hindrance on your path,
no shadow on your face,
until you lie down
in that mansion
in the arms of Christ benign.

Celtic

May the road rise to meet you.
May the wind be always at your back.
May the sun shine warm upon your face,
the rain fall soft upon your fields;
and until we meet again,
may God hold you
in the hollow of his hand.

Celtic

God's blessing be yours,
and well may it befall you;
Christ's blessing be yours,
and well be you entreated;
Spirit's blessing be yours
and well spend you your lives,
each day that you rise up,
each night that you lie down.

Celtic

The grace of God be with you,
the grace of Christ be with you,
the grace of the Spirit be with you
and with your children,
for an hour, for ever, for eternity.

Celtic

The keeping of the God of life be on you.
The keeping of the loving Christ be on you.
The keeping of the Holy Spirit be on you,
every night of your lives,
to aid you and enfold you,
each day and night of your lives.

Celtic

The peace of God be with you,
the peace of Christ be with you,
the peace of the Spirit be with you,
and with your children,
from this very day
to the last day of your lives,
until the very last day of your lives.

Celtic

May the everlasting Father himself
take you in his own generous clasp,
in his own generous arms.

Celtic

Deep peace of the running wave to you.
Deep peace of the flowing air to you.
Deep peace of the quiet earth to you.
Deep peace of the shining stars to you.
Deep peace of the Son of peace to you.
Celtic

Christ be with me, Christ within me,
Christ behind me, Christ before me,
Christ beside me, Christ to win me,
Christ to comfort and restore me,
Christ beneath me, Christ above me,
Christ in quiet, Christ in danger,
Christ in hearts of all that love me,
Christ in mouth of friend and stranger.
Attributed to St Patrick (c.386–c.460)
Translated by Cecil Frances Alexander (1818–1895)

My dearest Lord,
  be thou a bright flame before me,
  be thou a guiding star above me,
  be thou a smooth path beneath me,
  be thou a kindly shepherd behind me,
  today and evermore.
St Columba (521–597)

Give to us, O Lord,
  the peace of those who are glad to obey you,
  and the peace of those who rejoice in your praise,
  through Jesus Christ our Lord.
Amen.

St Aidan (d.651))

God be with you in every pass.
Jesus be with you on every hill.
Spirit be with you in every stream,
  headland, ridge and moor,
  each sea and land,
  each path and meadow,
  each lying down, each rising up,
  each step of the journey you take.

Gaelic

Offertory blessings

Lord we bring you these material gifts as a sign –
that all the world is yours,
and needs your blessing.
Peter Dainty

Loving Father,
you have given us all that you are, in Christ.
Help us, in Christ, to give all that we are to you.
Peter Dainty

We thank you, Lord, for all your gifts,
and dare to ask for one gift more –
the wisdom to use all these things aright,
through Jesus Christ our Lord.
Amen.
Peter Dainty

O Lord Jesus,
how pale are our offerings in the light of your cross.
Teach us to give as you give –
to make a sacrifice without counting the cost.
Peter Dainty

God, give us the faith to know
 that with our offerings
 you can do great things;
 but with our sacrifices
 you can work miracles.

Peter Dainty

Heavenly Father,
 we bring you these gifts of money as a sign –
 that even the great Mammon
 must bow the knee before the living God.

Peter Dainty

Lord God, by your grace
 help us to expend not only our money
 but our very selves
 in the service of your kingdom.

Peter Dainty

O God, we bring these gifts to you, and ask
 that the worship of our deeds
 may always more than match
 the worship of our words,
 through Jesus Christ our Lord.
Amen.

Peter Dainty

Loving God,
 may we learn from your generosity to us
 how to be more generous to our neighbours.

Peter Dainty

House and home

Father of all mankind,
make the roof of this house
wide enough for all opinions;
oil the door of this house
so that it opens easily
to friend and stranger;
and set such a table in this house
that all who come
may speak kindly and freely around it.

Hawaii

Christ's cross upon your new home.
Christ's cross upon your new hearth.
Christ's cross upon your new dwelling,
upon your new-kindled fire.

Christ's cross upon your tallest grass.
Christ's cross upon your fruitful partner.
Christ's cross upon your growing sons,
upon your growing daughters.

Christ's cross upon your household's helpers.
Christ's cross upon the children yet unborn.
Christ's cross upon the wise parents,
upon your occupation.

Christ's cross upon your goods and income.
Christ's cross upon your kith and kin.
Christ's cross upon you in light or in darkness,
each day and night of your lives.

Celtic

Bless, O God, the dwelling,
  and each who rest herein this night.
Bless, O God, my dear ones
  in every place wherein they sleep,
  in the night that is tonight,
  and every single night;
  in the day that is today,
  and every single day.

Celtic

Bless this house, O Lord, we pray;
  make it safe by night and day.
Bless these walls so firm and stout,
  keeping want and trouble out.
Bless the roof and chimneys tall,
  let thy peace lie over all.
Bless this door, that it may prove
  ever open to joy and love.

Bless these windows shining bright,
  letting in God's heavenly light.
Bless the hearth ablazing there,
  with smoke ascending like a prayer.
Bless the folk who dwell within;
  keep them pure and free from sin.
Bless us all that we may be
  fit, O Lord, to dwell with thee.
Bless us all that one day we
  may be fit to dwell, O Lord, with thee.

Helen Taylor (1893–1983)

The Sacred Three
  my fortress be
  encircling me.
Come and be round
  my hearth,
  my home.

Fend you my kin
  and every sleeping thing within
  from scathe, from sin.
Your care our peace
  through mid of night
  to night's release.

Alastair MacLean

Loved ones

God bless all those that I love.
God bless all those that love me.
God bless all those that love those that I love,
and all those that love those that love me.

On a New England sampler

Holy Father, in your mercy,
hear our earnest prayer:
keep our loved ones, now far distant,
'neath your care.

When in sorrow, when in danger,
when in loneliness,
in your love look down and comfort
their distress.

May the joy of your salvation
be their strength and stay;
may they love and may they praise you
day by day.

Isabel Stevenson (1843–1890)

Christ who first gave thee for a friend to me,
Christ keep thee well, where'er thou art, for me.
Earth's self shall go and the swift wheel of heaven
  perish and pass, before our love shall cease.
Do but remember me, as I do thee,
  and God, who brought us on this earth together,
  bring us together in his house of heaven.

Hrabanus Maurus (788–856)
to Grimold, Abbot of St Gall

Children

Almighty God
  and heavenly Father,
  we thank you for the children
  which you have given us.
Give us also wisdom to train them
  in your faith, fear and love,
  that as they advance in years,
  they may grow in grace,
  through Jesus Christ our Lord.
Amen.

Bishop Cosin (1595–1672)

Heavenly Father,
  bless our children
  with healthful bodies,
  with good understandings,
  with the graces and gifts
  of your Holy Spirit,
  with sweet dispositions
  and holy habits;
  and sanctify them throughout,
  in their bodies, souls and spirits,
  and keep them blameless
  to the coming
  of our Lord Jesus Christ.
Amen.

Jeremy Taylor (1613–1667)

The blessing of the Holy Three,
  little love, be the gift to thee:
  wisdom,
  peace
  and purity.

A Celtic prayer
which a mother whispers into the ear of her baby

Gentle Jesus, meek and mild,
  look upon this little child.
Pity *her* simplicity,
  suffer *her* to come to thee.
Let *her*, above all, fulfil
  God, *her* heavenly Father's will,
  never his good spirit grieve,
  only to his glory live.

Charles Wesley (1707–1788) alt.

New Year

Another year is dawning.
Dear Master, let it be,
  in working or in waiting,
  another year for thee:
  another year of mercies,
  of faithfulness and grace;
  another year of gladness
  in the shining of your face;
  another year of progress,
  another year of praise,
  another year of proving
  thy presence all our days;
  another year of service,
  of witness and of love;
  another year of training
  for holier work above.
Another year is dawning.
Dear Master, let it be,
  on earth, or else in heaven,
  another year for thee.
Amen.

Frances Ridley Havergal (1836–1879)

I said to the man who stood at the gate of the year:
'Give me a light, that I may tread safely
into the unknown.'
And he replied:
'Go out into the darkness
and put your hand into the hand of God.
That shall be to you better than light
and safer than a known way.'

New Year
Minnie Louise Haskins (1875–1957)

Lord, may the ticking of the clock on New Year's Eve
teach us to value every minute,
so that we waste no time on evil,
but grasp every opportunity for doing good.
May it teach us to value every hour:
especially the hour of prayer
when we watch with Jesus,
and the hour of the kingdom
when we rejoice with him.
May it teach us to value every day,
for now is the day of salvation,
and today is always the Day of the Lord.
And may it remind us
that though we live in a world of time,
every second is a meeting point with eternity.

Peter Dainty

Infant baptism

Lord Jesus Christ, our Lord most dear,
as you were once an infant here,
so give this child of yours, we pray,
your grace and blessing day by day.

Their watch let angels round *him* keep
where'er *he* be, awake, asleep.
Be pleased your caring love to give,
and keep this child by morn and eve.

As in your heavenly kingdom, Lord,
all things obey your sacred word,
may *he* your holy cross so bear
that with your saints a crown *he'll* wear.

Heinrich von Laufenberg (Fifteenth century)
Translated by Catherine Winkworth (1827–1878) alt.

Jesus, may *(name)* always know
the joys of loving and being loved.
May *she* never know
what it is to be lonely.
May *she* be generous
and compassionate
and quick to understand and respond
to the needs of others.
May the world be a better place
for *her* presence in it.
Amen.

Susan Hardwick

Jesus, may *(name)* grow in
  knowledge and love of you each day.
May every step of *his* life
  be walked along your way.
Watch over *him* and guide *him*
  to know you as *his* Lord and Saviour.

Heavenly Father, give (*name*)
  a deep love of learning,
  and the wisdom to understand
  how to use the knowledge *he* gains.
May he know the joy of curiosity
  and wonder in your beautiful world.
May *he* never stop asking questions.

Lord of all, bless (*name*) with a
  deep sense of joy and happiness
  throughout *his* life.
When times are hard –
  as sometimes they will be –
  may *he* still have a thankful heart
  for blessings received
  and for your faithful presence.
Amen.

Susan Hardwick

God of all, guide *(name)*
along the path of life
you have chosen for *her.*
May *she* greet each bright new day
with joy and excitement
at all that it might bring.
May she always
be filled with wonder.
May she always
walk with you.
Amen.

Susan Hardwick

God, make this child a shining light
within the world to glow,
a little flame that burneth bright,
wherever *he* may go.
God, make *his* life a joyful song
that comforteth the sad,
that helpeth others to be strong
and makes the singer glad.
God, make *his* life a trusty staff,
whereon the weak may rest,
so that what health and strength *he* hath
may serve *his* neighbours best.
God, make *his* life a constant hymn
of wonder and of praise,
of faith and hope that never dim
and love in all his ways.

Matilda Barbara Bethan-Edwards (1836–1919) alt.

Adult baptism and confirmation

Lord, let your grace descend on those,
who, hoping in your word,
this day do publicly declare
that Jesus is their Lord.

With cheerful feet may they advance,
and run the Christian race;
and through the troubles of the way
find all-sufficient grace.

James Newton (1732–1790)

Stand, soldier of the cross,
your high allegiance claim,
and vow to hold the world but loss
for your redeemer's name.

No more your own, but Christ's –
with all the saints of old,
apostles, seers, evangelists,
and martyr throngs enrolled.

In God's whole armour strong,
front hell's embattled powers;
the warfare may be sharp and long,
but vict'ry must be ours.

E. H. Bickersteth (1825–1906)

Marriage

May you know length of life
  and sun-filled days,
  and may you not have to depart this life
  before your own child falls in love.
Traditional Irish

O God of love, to you we bow,
  and humbly pray before you now,
  for those who make their marriage vow:
  may they in you be one.

When days are filled with pure delight,
  when paths are plain and skies are bright,
  walking by faith and not by sight,
  may they in you be one.

When stormy winds fulfil your will,
  and all their good seems turned to ill,
  then, trusting you completely, still
  may they in you be one.

Whate'er in life shall be their share
  of quickening joy or burdening care,
  in power to do and grace to bear,
  may they in you be one.

Eternal love, with them abide;
  in you for ever may they hide,
  for even death cannot divide
  those who have been made one.

William Vaughan Jenkins (1868–1920) alt.

O perfect Love,
all human thought transcending,
lowly we kneel in prayer
before your throne,
that theirs may be the love,
which knows no ending,
who in your love
for evermore are one.

O perfect Life,
be now their full assurance
of tender charity
and steadfast faith,
of patient hope,
and quiet brave endurance,
with childlike trust
that fears not pain or death.

Grant them the joy
which brightens earthly sorrow.
Grant them the peace,
which calms all earthly strife;
and to life's day
the glorious unknown morrow
that dawns upon eternal love and life.

Dorothy Francis Gurney (1858–1932)

Let Love rule in your lives,
  and make you one.
Let Love rule everything –
  all joys and pleasures,
  and all grief and pain;
  times of excitement and delight,
  and everyday routine.
Let Love rule in your minds,
  that all your thoughts
  be for the other's good,
  and not their ill.
Let Love reign in your bodies,
  so that you may share your passions
  with an equal ecstasy;
  but with no other.
And if Love truly reigns within your hearts,
  though trials come
  which tempt you both to part,
  you never will.
So let Love rule, and you'll know then,
  that I'll be with you both,
  for evermore.
Amen.

God's Marriage Blessing
Peter Dainty

Education

Loving God, bless (*name)*
as *he* goes to school today (for the first time).
May *he* soon make friends by being friendly,
find his way around by being ready to ask,
settle into the routine by listening to instructions,
enjoy the lessons by being eager to learn,
get on well with the other children and the teachers
by being cheerful, helpful and polite,
and make the most of every opportunity
by doing *his* very best.
May *he* be keen to go to school every morning
and happy when *he* comes home in the afternoon,
so that *he* will come to remember *his* schooldays
as the happiest days of *his* life – so far.

Starting school
Peter Dainty

O God our Father, be with us
as we return to school
refreshed and revitalised by the holidays,
and ready to begin a new year.
Give us the energy and enthusiasm
to make the most of every opportunity
that school provides,
to develop our interests, abilities, and skills,
to grow in knowledge and understanding,
and to get on well with others.

May we work hard and play fair.
May we enjoy what is good
and learn from what goes wrong,
so that we come to the end of each day
with a satisfying sense of achievement.
God bless our school.

The start of the year
Peter Dainty

Heavenly Father,
as we come to the end
of a busy term,
we thank you for all the good experiences
of the past weeks and months –
the things we've enjoyed,
the things we've achieved
and the things we've learned,
especially what we've learned
even from bad experiences.
We thank you for old friendships reinforced,
and new friendships made.
Now bless all these things to our good,
and send us on our way
to enjoy the holiday to the full.

End of term
Peter Dainty

Lord God, bless all those
  who are taking examinations today.
May they have the confidence of knowing
  that they have prepared
  as thoroughly as they can.
Take away their anxiety,
  so that they may be able to concentrate
  and do themselves justice.
And may each one be rewarded
  with the result they deserve.

Taking examinations
Peter Dainty

Lord, be with me as I start college/university.
Help me through all its waiting experiences –
  studying new subjects in greater depth,
  meeting new people from many places,
  enjoying new activities and developing old ones.
Through all the excitement and challenge,
  the freedom and responsibilities,
  the stresses and temptations
  of student life,
  help me to grow up in mind and spirit,
  and to stand firm in faith,
  knowing that you are with me always,
  Jesus Christ my Lord.
Amen.

Going to college or university
Peter Dainty

God bless all those who teach
  in schools, colleges and universities.
May their own enthusiasm for their subject
  rub off on those they teach.
May they expect high standards of work and learning,
  and know how to praise enthusiastically
  as well as criticise creatively.
May they always have the best interest of their students
  at heart,
  and have a sensitive pastoral concern
  for their students' needs and problems.
Give them knowledge and skill,
  but also give them grace, wisdom, patience
  and understanding.

Teachers
Peter Dainty

Work

Lord, help me in my daily work,
both when I enjoy it
and when I don't,
when I am full of energy and enthusiasm,
and when I am not.
May I be able to take pride
in knowing that I am doing something useful,
something that is of service to others,
and of benefit to the community.
May I be pleasant and cheerful,
both with my fellow workers,
and with those whom I serve.
May I be conscientious, honest and reliable,
and keen to develop my knowledge and skill;
for the sake of Jesus the Carpenter.
Amen.

Peter Dainty

O Lord, thou knowest how busy I must be this day;
if I forget thee, do not thou forget me.

General Lord Astley (1579–1652)

God, bless us in our work.
You called Matthew from his tax collecting
  and Peter, Andrew, James and John from their fishing,
  but help us to serve you *in* our occupations.
In the name of Joseph the carpenter
  and Paul the tentmaker,
  bless us as we earn a living
  to support our families,
  and work to serve the needs of others.
May we never be afraid
  to get our hands dirty
  in honest labour,
  to go out of our way
  to be kind and helpful,
  or to spend long hours
  in doing a job well.
God, you have given us work to do;
  help us to do it as if for you.
Amen.

Peter Dainty

Our country

God bless our native land!
May heaven's protective hand
still guard our shore.
May peace her power extend,
foe be transformed to friend,
and Britain's rights depend
on war no more.

O Lord, our monarch bless
with strength and righteousness;
long may she reign.
Her heart inspire and move
with wisdom from above,
and in a nation's love
her throne maintain.

May just and righteous laws
uphold the public cause,
under God's hand.
Home of the brave and free,
nation of liberty,
built on democracy –
God bless this land!

And not this land alone,
but be God's mercies known
from shore to shore.
Lord, may all nations see
that we should brothers be,
and form one family
the wide world o'er.

William Edward Hickson (1803–1870) alt.

Lord, while for all mankind we pray,
  of every clime and coast,
  O hear us for our native land,
  the land we love the most.

Our fathers' sepulchres are here,
  and here our kindred dwell,
  our children too; how should we love
  another land so well?

Lord, guard our shores from every foe;
  with peace our borders bless;
  with prosperous times our cities crown,
  our fields with plenteousness.

Unite us in the sacred love
  of knowledge, truth, and thee;
  and let our hills and valleys shout
  the songs of liberty.

Lord of the nations, thus to thee
  our country we commend;
  be thou her refuge and her trust,
  her everlasting friend.

John Reynell Wreford (1800–1881)

Travellers

To thy Fatherly protection, O Lord,
  we commend ourselves and those about to travel.
Bless, guide, and defend us,
  that we may so pass through this world
  as finally to enjoy in thy presence
  everlasting happiness, for Jesus Christ's sake.
Amen.

Dr Samuel Johnson (1709–1784)

He who directs the sparrow's tender flight,
  and sees him safely reach the heartless ground,
  guide thee in all thy passages aright,
  and grant thy course be sure, thy resting sound.

Air Travellers
Richard Zouche (1590–1661)

Life's journey

May our loving heavenly Father
guide and keep you in his care.
May the blessings of his Holy Spirit
all be yours to share.
May God's wisdom be the light that
leads your footsteps every day,
and his presence your companion
as you walk along life's way.

Anon

O Lord God, when thou givest to thy servants
to endeavour any great matter,
grant us also to know that it is not the beginning,
but the continuing of the same,
until it be thoroughly finished,
which yieldeth the true glory;
through him who, for the finishing of thy work,
laid down his life for us,
our Redeemer, Jesus Christ.
Amen.

Attributed to Sir Francis Drake (1540–1596)

Give me my scallop-shell of quiet,
my staff of faith to walk upon,
my scrip of joy, immortal diet,
my bottle of salvation,
my gown of glory, hope's true gage;
and thus I'll take my pilgrimage.

Blood must be my body's balmer;
no other balm will there be given;
whilst my soul, like quiet palmer,
travelleth towards the land of heaven,
over the silver mountains,
where spring the nectar fountains.
There I will kiss
the bowl of bliss;
and drink mine everlasting fill
upon every milken hill.
My soul will be a-dry before;
but after, it will thirst no more.

His Pilgrimage
Sir Walter Raleigh (1552–1618)

Praise be to you, our God, this day;
lead us along your holy way,
that guided by your heavenly light
we'll see the truth and do the right;
through Jesus Christ, our Lord.
Amen.

Peter Dainty

Benedictions at the close of worship

May God, the Lord, bless us
with all heavenly benediction,
and make us pure and holy in his sight.
May the riches of his glory abound in us.
May he instruct us with the word of truth,
inform us with the Gospel of salvation
and enrich us with his love,
through Jesus Christ our Lord.
Amen.

Gelasian Sacramentary

Lord, dismiss us with your blessing,
fill our hearts with joy and peace.
Let us each, your love possessing,
triumph in redeeming grace.
O refresh us, O refresh us,
travelling through this wilderness.

Thanks we give, and adoration,
for your gospel's joyful sound.
May the fruits of your salvation
in our hearts and lives abound.
May your presence, may your presence
with us evermore be found.

John Fawcett (1740–1817)

May the Lord lead us when we go,
and keep us when we sleep,
and talk with us when we wake;
and may the peace of God
which passes all understanding
keep our hearts and minds in Christ Jesus, our Lord.

Anon

May our Lord Jesus Christ be near to defend us,
within us to refresh us,
around us to preserve us,
before us to guide us,
behind us to justify us,
above us to bless us;
who lives and reigns
with the Father and the Holy Ghost,
God for evermore.
Amen.

Anon (Tenth century)

May God the Father bless us.
May Christ the Son take care of us.
May the Holy Ghost enlighten us,
all the days of our life.
The Lord be our defender of body and soul
both now and for ever to the ages of ages.
Amen.

Anon

Keep us in peace, O Christ our God,
under the protection
of your holy and venerable cross.
Save us from our enemies,
visible and invisible,
and count us worthy
to glorify you with thanksgiving,
with the Father and the Holy Spirit,
now and for ever,
world without end.
Amen.

Armenian Orthodox

Forth in thy name, O Lord, we go,
our daily labour to pursue;
you, only you, resolved to know
in all we think, or speak, or do.

The task your wisdom has assigned
O let us cheerfully fulfil;
in all our works your presence find
and prove your good and perfect will.

Give us to bear your easy yoke,
and every moment watch and pray,
and still to things eternal look,
and hasten to your glorious day.

For you delightfully employ
whate'er your bounteous grace has given,
and run our course with even joy,
and closely walk with you to heaven.

Charles Wesley (1707–1788) alt.

The Lord bless us and keep us.
The Spirit of the Lord cleanse and purify our inmost hearts
  and enable us to shun all evil.
The Lord enlighten our understanding
  and cause the light of truth to shine into our hearts.
The Lord fill us with faith and love towards him.
The Lord be with us day and night,
  in our coming in and our going out,
  in our sorrow and in our joy
  and bring us at length into his eternal rest.
Amen.

Anon

The peace of God,
  which passeth all understanding,
  keep your hearts and minds
  in the knowledge and love of God,
  and of his Son, Jesus Christ our Lord.
And the blessing of God Almighty,
  Father, Son and Holy Ghost,
  be amongst you and remain with you always.

Holy Communion 1549

May the eternal God bless us and keep us,
  guard our bodies, save our souls, direct our thoughts
  and bring us safe to the heavenly country,
  our eternal home
  where Father, Son and Holy Spirit ever reign,
  one God for ever and ever.

The Sarum Breviary

May the grace of Christ our Saviour
  and the Father's boundless love,
  with the Holy Spirit's favour,
  rest upon us from above.
Thus may we abide in union
  with each other and the Lord,
  and possess, in sweet communion,
  joys which earth cannot afford.

John Newton (1725–1807)

May the Lord bless you with all good
  and keep you from all evil.
May he give light to your heart with loving wisdom,
  and be gracious to you with eternal knowledge.
May he lift up his eternal countenance upon you
  for eternal peace.

The Dead Sea Scrolls

The blessing of the Lord
  rest and remain upon all his people,
  in every land, of every tongue.
The Lord meet in mercy all that seek him.
The Lord comfort all who suffer and mourn.
The Lord hasten his coming,
  and give us the blessing of peace.

Handley Moule (1841–1920)

May the Lord bless you and protect you.
May the Lord smile upon you and show you his favour.
May the Lord befriend you and prosper you.

Anon
cf Numbers 6:24-26

May the love of the Father enfold us,
the wisdom of the Son enlighten us,
the fire of the Spirit inflame us;
and may the blessing of the triune God
rest upon us, and abide within us,
now and evermore.

Anon

Eternal Light, shine into our hearts.
Eternal Goodness, deliver our thoughts from evil.
Eternal Power, support our prayer.
Eternal Wisdom, enlighten the darkness of our ignorance.
Eternal Pity, have mercy upon us;
that with all our heart and mind and soul and strength
we may seek thy face,
and be brought by thine infinite mercy
to thy holy presence; through Jesus Christ our Lord.
Amen.

Alcuin of York (735–804)

Spirit of truth, fill our minds.
Spirit of Christ, fill our hearts.
Spirit of power and holiness, revive your Church.
Spirit of love, bind us together in Christian fellowship.
Spirit of justice and peace,
  lead all nations into your kingdom.
In the name of Jesus.
Amen.

Peter Dainty

Bless us, O Lord,
  through your holy feasts,
  and fill us with living joy
  and peace in our hearts.
Bless us now and always,
  and make us holy
  as we obey your holy law.
Fill us with your goodness
  and gladden our souls
  with your salvation.
Purify our hearts
  as we serve you in love and truth
  and welcome with joy and gratitude
  your holy festivals.

A Jewish Prayer for Festivals from the Talmud

May the Lord Jesus Christ fill us with spiritual joy.
May his Spirit make us strong and tranquil
in the truths of his promises.
And may the blessing of the Lord
come upon us abundantly.
Amen.

Anon

May God, the fountain of all blessing,
fill us with the understanding of sacred knowledge.
May he keep us sound in faith, steadfast in hope,
and persevering in patient charity.
And may the blessing of the Father, the Son
and the Holy Spirit,
and the peace of the Lord be with us always.
Amen.

Anon

May our blessed Lord be with us,
and the love of the eternal Father follow us.
The mighty Saviour be our Shepherd and defence.
The Holy Spirit sanctify, counsel and confirm us,
for the praise of him
who is called into his marvellous light,
and into the footsteps of him who is the Way,
the Truth, and the Life,
even Jesus Christ our Lord.
Amen.

Anon

Eternal God, the light of the minds that know you,
the joy of the hearts that love you,
and the strength of the wills that serve you;
grant us to know you
that we may truly love you;
so to love you that we may fully serve you,
to the honour and glory of your Holy Name.
Amen.

The Gelasian Sacramentary,
based on the words of St Augustine

May the blessing of God Almighty,
the Father, the Son and the Holy Spirit,
rest upon us and upon all our work and worship
done in his name.
May he give us light to guide us,
courage to support us,
love to unite us,
now and for evermore.
Amen.

Anon

May the grace of Christ uphold us.
May the Father's love enfold us.
May the Holy Spirit guide us,
so that, with the Lord beside us,
we may go our way in peace.
Amen.

Peter Dainty

At the end of the day

Grant us thy peace upon our homeward way;
with thee began, with thee shall end the day.
Guard thou the lips from sin, the hearts from shame,
that in this house have called upon thy name.

Grant us thy peace, Lord, through the coming night;
turn thou for us its darkness into light.
From harm and danger keep thy children free,
for dark and light are both alike to thee.

Grant us thy peace throughout our earthly life,
our balm in sorrow and our stay in strife.
Then, when thy voice shall bid our conflict cease,
call us, O Lord, to thine eternal peace.

John Ellerton (1826–1893)

God be in my head
and in my understanding.
God be in my eyes
and in my looking.
God be in my mouth
and in my speaking.
God be in my heart
and in my thinking.
God be at my end
and at my departing.

Book of Hours, 1514

God guide us waking
and guard us sleeping,
that awake we may watch with Christ,
and asleep we may rest in peace.
Susan Sayers

O God, our help in ages past,
our hope for years to come,
be thou our guard while life shall last,
and our eternal home
Isaac Watts (1674 1748)

Lord, keep us safe this night,
secure from all our fears;
may angels guard us while we sleep,
till morning light appears.
Source unknown

Day is done.
Gone the sun,
from the lake,
from the hills,
from the sky.
Safely rest.
All is well.
God is nigh.
Anon

Matthew, Mark, Luke and John
  bless the bed that I lie on.
Before I lay me down to sleep,
  I pray the Lord my soul to keep.

I go by sea, I go by land;
  the Lord made me with his right hand.
Should any danger come to me,
  sweet Jesus Christ deliver me.

He's the branch and I'm the flower,
  pray God send me a happy hour.
And should I die before I wake,
  I pray the Lord my soul to take.

Four corners to my bed,
  four angels there are spread;
  two at the foot, two at the head:
  four to carry me when I'm dead.

Bedtime Prayer
Anon

Goodnight! Goodnight! Far flies the light.
But still God's love shall shine above,
  making all bright. Goodnight! Goodnight!

Victor Hugo (1802–1885)

O Lord, who by your presence have made light
the heat and burden of the toilsome day,
be with us also in the silent night,
be with us when the daylight fades away.

Come then, O Lord, and deign to be our Guest,
after the day's confusion, toil, and din.
O come to bring us peace and joy and rest,
to give salvation, and to pardon sin.

Bind up the wounds, assuage the aching smart
left in our feelings from the day just past;
and let us on the Father's loving heart
forget our griefs, and find sweet rest at last.

Carl Johann Philipp Spitta (1801–1859)
Translated by Richard Massie (1800–1887) alt.

Through life's long day and death's dark night,
O gentle Jesus, be our light.

Frederick William Faber (1814–1863)

God the Father, be thou near;
save us from every harm tonight.
Make us all thy children dear,
in the darkness be our light.

God the Saviour, be our peace;
put away our sins tonight.
Speak the word of full release;
turn our darkness into light.

Holy Spirit, deign to come;
sanctify us all tonight.
In our hearts prepare thy home;
turn our darkness into light.

Holy Trinity, be nigh,
mystery of love adored.
Help to live, and help to die;
lighten all our darkness, Lord.

George Rawson (1807–1889)

Departing

Bring us, O Lord our God, at our last awakening,
into the house and gate of heaven,
to enter into that gate and dwell in that house,
where there shall be no darkness or dazzling,
but one equal light;
no noise or silence,
but one equal music;
no fears or hopes,
but one equal possession;
no ends or beginnings,
but one equal eternity;
in the habitations of thy glory and dominion,
world without end.

John Donne (1572–1631)

Go forth upon your journey, Christian soul,
go from this world.
Go in the name of God, the omnipotent Father,
who created you.
Go in the name of Jesus Christ our Lord,
who died for you.
Go in the name of the Holy Spirit,
who hath been poured out on you,
and will sustain us both until we meet again.
May God be with you till we meet again.

The Dream of Gerontius
John Henry Newman (1801–1890)

As you were before me, at my life's beginning,
  be so again, at my journey's end.

As you were beside me, at my soul's shaping,
  Father, be there with me, at my journey's close.

Celtic

God be with you till we meet again;
  by his counsels guide, uphold you,
  with his sheep securely fold you.
God be with you till we meet again.

God be with you till we meet again;
  'neath his wings protecting hide you,
  daily manna still provide you.
God be with you till we meet again.

God be with you till we meet again;
  when life's perils thick confound you,
  put his arms unfailing round you.
God be with you till we meet again.

God be with you till we meet again;
  keep love's banner floating o'er you,
  smite death's threatening wave before you.
God be with you till we meet again.

Jeremiah Eames Rankin (1828–1904)

Pray for me, as I will for thee,
  that we may merrily meet in heaven.

Thomas More (1478–1535)

GRACES

General graces

God, bless this food to our use, and us to your service.
Amen.

Anon

Benedictus, benedicat,
per Jesum Christum Dominum nostrum.

A Latin grace

Be present at our table, Lord,
  be here and everywhere adored.
Thy creatures bless, and grant that we
  may feast in paradise with thee.

John Cennick (1718–1755)

Great God and giver of all good,
  accept our praise and bless our food.
Grace, health and strength to us afford
  through Jesus Christ, our risen Lord.

Jeremiah Clarke (1674–1707)

May the food we eat restore our strength,
give new energy to tired limbs,
and new thoughts to tired minds.
May our drink restore our souls,
give new vision to dry spirits,
and new warmth to cold hearts.
And when we are refreshed,
may we give new pleasure to you,
who gives us all.

A Celtic grace

We thank you, Lord,
for your good gifts –
for good food,
for good friends / company,
and for good conversation –
and we ask your blessing on this meal,
through Jesus Christ our Lord.
Amen.

Peter Dainty

Heavenly Father,
we accept with gratitude
the gifts you have bestowed on us today
through the love and skill of *(name those who prepared the meal).*

From Oberammergau

Lord, Christ, we pray thy mercy on our table spread;
and what thy gentle hands have given us,
let it be blessed.

Alcuin of York (753–804)

May the blessing of the five loaves and two fishes,
which the Lord shared out among the five thousand,
be ours.
May the king who did the sharing bless our sharing.

A Celtic grace

Thank you for the world so sweet.
Thank you for the food we eat.
Thank you for the birds that sing.
Thank you, God, for everything.

Edith Rutter Leadham (c.1908)

Come, Lord Jesus, be our guest,
and may our meal by thee be blest.

Attributed to Martin Luther (1483–1546)

To God, who gives our daily bread,
a thankful song we raise,
and pray that he who sends us food
may fill our hearts with praise.

Thomas Tallis (1510–1585)

You who give food to all flesh,
who feed the young ravens that cry to you
and have nourished us from our youth up:
fill our hearts with good and gladness
and strengthen us with your grace.

Lancelot Andrewes (1555–1626)

Pray we to God, the Almighty Lord,
that sendeth food to beasts and men,
to send his blessing on this board,
to feed us now and evermore – Amen.

From an Elizabethan Book of Private Prayer (1553)

The eyes of all things look up and trust in you, O Lord.
You give them their meat in due season.
You open your hand and fill with your blessing
every living thing.
Good Lord, bless us and all the good things
which we receive
of your bountiful liberality;
through Jesus Christ our Lord.

Queen Elizabeth I (1533–1603)

We give you thanks, O Lord our God,
for earthly and for heavenly food:
for that which makes our bodies whole,
and that which satisfies the soul.
Bless this our meal, and give us grace
to share our joys in love and peace.

Peter Dainty

For life, and love, and home, and food;
for daily bread and holy word;
for all you give us for our good;
we thank you, heavenly Father.

Peter Dainty

Lord, bless the food which now we take,
and make us strong, for Jesus' sake.

Anon

Bless me, O Lord,
and let my food strengthen me to serve you,
for Jesus Christ's sake.

Isaac Watts (1674–1748)

We thank you, Lord, for daily bread,
our bodies and our souls to feed.
We ask for strength to do your will,
and pray for those in special need.

Peter Dainty

For love and joy, for home and friends,
for all that binds and all that mends,
for every gift that heaven sends,
we give you thanks, our Father.

Peter Dainty

Father, give us food each day
  to keep us well and strong,
  that we may use our health and strength
  to please you all day long.

Anon

Let us, with gladsome mind,
  praise the Lord, for he is kind.
All things living he doth feed;
  his full hand supplies their need.

John Milton (1608–1674)

For these and all thy mercies given,
  we thank you, heavenly Father.

Anon

What God gives, and what we take,
  'tis a gift for Christ his sake;
be the meal of beans and peas,
  God be thanked for those and these.
Have we flesh, or have we fish,
  all are fragments from his dish.
He his Church save, and the king,
  and our peace here, like a spring,
  make it ever flourishing.

Robert Herrick (1591–1674)

Give us this day our daily bread,
for by your grace we all are fed.

Anon

For rest and food and work to do,
for family love and friendship true,
for all that makes us turn to you,
we thank you, heavenly Father.

Peter Dainty

Thy glory here we make our aim,
to eat and drink in Jesu's name
nor live to eat but eat to live,
our food we now with thanks receive.

Charles Wesley (1707–1788)

Almighty King, whose wondrous hand,
supports the weight of sea and land,
whose grace is such a boundless store,
no heart shall break that sighs for more.
Thy providence supplies my food,
and 'tis thy blessing makes it good.
My soul is nourished by thy Word,
let soul and body praise the Lord.

William Cowper (1731–1800)

We thank you, Lord, for food and drink
 which give us health and energy.
May we not eat what is not good,
 nor waste our days in lethargy.

Peter Dainty

Thou that has given so much to me,
 give one thing more – a grateful heart;
 not thankful when it pleases me,
 as if thy blessings had spare days;
 but such a heart, whose very pulse
 may be thy praise.

George Herbert (1593–1633)

For what we are about to receive,
 may the Lord make us truly thankful.

Anon

We thank you, Father,
 that we have enough bread for today;
 and we trust you that when the time comes
 we shall have enough bread for tomorrow also.

Peter Dainty

Be known to us in breaking bread,
  but do not then depart.
Saviour, abide with us, and spread
  your table in our heart.

James Montgomery (1771–1854)

Glory, love, and praise, and honour,
  for our food now bestowed
  render we the donor.

Knows the ox his master's stable,
  and shall we not know thee,
  nourished at this table?

Yes, of all good gifts the Giver,
  thee we own, thee alone
  magnify for ever.

Charles Wesley (1707–1788), adapted

We thank you for fresh food each day;
  for you, our God, make all things new.
While eating, may we realise
  how much we all depend on you.

Peter Dainty

Thankful for our every blessing,
  let us sing Christ the spring
  never, never ceasing.
Source of all our gifts and graces,
  Christ we own, Christ alone
  calls for all our praises.

He dispels our sins and sadness,
  life imparts, cheers our hearts,
  fills with food and gladness.
Who himself for all has given,
  us he feeds, us he leads
  to a feast in heaven.

Charles Wesley (1707–1788)

All good gifts around us
  are sent from heaven above.
Then thank the Lord, O thank the Lord,
  for all his love.

Matthias Claudius (1740–1815)
Translated by Jane Montgomery Campbell (1817–1878)

Biblical graces

It is right that we should rejoice on this holy day,
by eating and drinking,
and sharing God's good gifts with others.
Let us praise God together,
for the joy of the Lord is our strength.

Based on Nehemiah 8:10-12

For this splendid meal, we thank the Lord.
The food looks delicious and the drink refreshing.
So let us taste and see that the Lord is good.

Based on Psalm 34:8

Let us eat bread with joy
and drink wine with a merry heart,
for God wants us to enjoy his gifts.

Based on Ecclesiastes 9:7

Bless the Lord, O my soul;
  and all that is within me, bless his holy name!
Bless the Lord, O my soul,
  and forget not all his benefits...
  who satisfies you with good as long as you live
  so that your youth is renewed like the eagle's.

Psalm 103:1, 2, 5 (RSV)

Let us thank the Lord for his unfailing love,
  and also for his wonderful works,
  for he satisfies those who thirst,
  and fills the hungry with good things.

Psalm 107:8, 9

Lord, bless your rich creation,
  and feed the poor with more than bread.

Based on Psalm 132:15

All eyes, O Lord, look up to you,
  to give them food when time is due.
They watch your full hand opening
  to nourish every living thing.
You see their need. You hear their cry.
Thanks be to you, Lord God most high.

Based on Psalm 145:15, 16, 18, 19

We thank you, Father, for our earthly bread,
which meets our earthly need.
We thank you also for the Bread from heaven,
on which our spirits feed –
Jesus, the Bread of Life.
Amen.

Based on John 6:27, 31-35

Jesus, Bread of Life,
feed us that we may truly live.

John 6:51

Lord, we consecrate this food with prayer;
for all that you have made is good,
to be received with thanksgiving.
Thanks be to God.
Amen.

1 Timothy 4:4, 5

Humorous graces

For every cup and plateful,
Lord, make us truly grateful.

Anon

Give thanks to God for the things he's made –
for cornflakes, tea and marmalade;
for bacon and eggs and butter and toast
praise Father, Son and Holy Ghost.

Anon

Lord, do not make us like porridge – thick, stodgy,
hard to stir and lacking in taste.
Make us like cornflakes – crisp, fresh
and ready to serve.

Anon

Lord, grant that we may not be like cornflakes –
lightweight, brittle and cold.
Make us like porridge – warm, comforting
and full of natural goodness.

Anon

As Jesus blessed the loaves and fishes,
God, be pleased to bless these dishes.

Peter Dainty

Ta, Pa.
Anon

G, thanks.
Anon

God, bless this bunch
as they munch their lunch.
Anon

Give me a good digestion, Lord,
  and also something to digest;
give me a healthy body, Lord,
  with sense to keep it at its best.
Chester Cathedral

Some have meat, and cannot eat,
  some cannot eat that want it.
But we have meat, and we can eat,
  sae let the Lord be thankit.
Robert Burns (1759–1796)

For rabbits young and rabbits old;
  for rabbits hot and rabbits cold;
  for rabbits tender, rabbits tough,
  we thank thee, Lord, we've had enough.
Attributed to Jonathan Swift (1667–1745)

With chicken stew and chicken roast,
and chicken leg and chicken breast,
and chicken soup and fricassee,
thank God we don't have chicken tea.

Peter Dainty
after Jonathan Swift

Here a little child I stand,
heaving up my either hand:
cold as paddocks* though they be,
here I lift them up to thee,
for a benison to fall
on our meat and on our all.

Robert Herrick (1591–1674)

Heavenly Father, keep us alive:
there's ten of us for dinner,
and grub for only five.

Rural Suffolk (Nineteenth century)

We thank you that the food was quick,
and ask that it won't make us sick.

In a fast food restaurant
Peter Dainty

**Frogs and toads*

For particular occasions

O give thanks to him, who made
morning light and evening shade,
source and giver of all good,
nightly sleep, and daily food;
quickener of our wearied powers,
guard of our unconscious hours.
Amen.

Breakfast
Josiah Conder (1789–1855)

Another day is dawning;
another table spread.
Lord make us truly grateful
for this our daily bread.

Breakfast
Anon

For each new morning with its light,
for rest and shelter of the night,
for health and food, for love and friends,
for everything thy goodness sends:
accept our thanks, O Lord.

Breakfast
Ralph Waldo Emerson (1803–1882)

At breakfast time we give you thanks
for night's long sleep and morning's light.
Now give us energy for work,
to seek what's good and do what's right.

Breakfast
Peter Dainty

For sleep throughout night past,
for light at break of day,
for food to break our fast
and strength to work and play,
we thank you, God our Father.

Breakfast
Peter Dainty

Lord, bless this food and this company.
May we take pleasure in eating and drinking,
in conversation and laughter,
as we celebrate your goodness and love
on this special occasion.

Any special occasion
Peter Dainty

For this season of loving, and sharing, and giving,
and all the good things that make life worth living,
we praise you, Christ, our Saviour.

A Christmas grace
Peter Dainty

Lord Jesus, may we celebrate your birth
with the joy of the angels,
the generosity of the wise men
and the excitement of the shepherds.
But save us from the extravagance
which makes us forget
that Jesus was born in a stable.

A Christmas grace
Peter Dainty

Let not our hearts be busy inns
that have no room for thee,
but cradles of the living Christ
and his nativity.

Welsh

Lord, teach us how to fast during Lent
with shining faces, glad hearts
and the happiness that comes
from meeting the needs of others.

A Lenten grace
Peter Dainty

Hunger and thirst, O Christ,
for sight of thee,
came between me
and all the feasts of earth.
Give thou thyself to me –
thyself the Bread,
thyself the Wine.
Thou art our sole provision for the unknown way,
long hunger wasteth those
who wander through the world.
With sight of thee may we be satisfied.

A Lenten grace
Radbod: Bishop of Utrecht (c.900)

We thank you, Lord,
that you have said
we cannot live by bread alone.
So give us grace to seek what's good
and feed upon your heavenly word,
and make its truth our own.

A Lenten grace
Peter Dainty

As we thank you for your gifts on this solemn day,
help us to remember that,
just as our eternal salvation has been won for us
by the self-giving and sacrifice of Christ,
so our daily survival is made possible
by the service, self-giving and sacrifice of others.
Amen.

A Good Friday grace
Peter Dainty

Risen Lord,
we celebrate the joy of Easter today,
by sharing not only our food
but our faith and joy
because you have triumphed over sin and death.
Hallelujah!

An Easter grace
Peter Dainty

Lord Jesus,
as you surprised your friends
by appearing among them
and sharing food with them
at that first Easter time,
so come to be our guest today,
and live in our hearts for ever.

An Easter grace
Peter Dainty

Loving Father,
we thank you for (*baby's name),*
your precious gift to us.
And we thank you that *he/she*
has been baptised today,
and welcomed into the family of your Church.
So we celebrate together
in the pleasure
of this family-gathering
with food and drink,
laughter and conversation.
May (*baby's name*) enjoy it too
and one day be glad to know
that this was the beginning
of *his/her* Christian pilgrimage.
Amen.

A Christening party
Peter Dainty

King of creation, we bless you for
the love that comes to flower this day,
the earth that brings us this food,
the friendship that has drawn this company together.
May we feast in the presence of our eternal host,
bringing cupfuls of kindness and platefuls of love.

A wedding grace
Ray Simpson

We thank you, Lord,
 that we are able to share in the happiness
 of (*name*) and (*name*)
 as we celebrate their marriage in this meal together.
We pray for your blessing on them and their families,
 both now, and in the years to come.

A wedding grace
Peter Dainty

A wedding is a cause for celebration,
 for praising God that two are joined as one,
 their lives so intertwined that joys are doubled,
 but pain and stress are never borne alone.

And silver is a thing of worth and beauty,
 symbol of what we value most in life:
 relationships of faithfulness and sharing,
 family bonds, the love of man and wife.

A silver wedding, then, is extra special,
 a time of thanks for five and twenty years
 in which those things that matter have been moulded,
 refined in fires of love, tempered with tears.

Our prayer for you is simple, (*name*) and (*name*):
 may love grow deeper still as years unfold,
 and may God's grace, which first brought you together,
 transmute your precious silver into gold.

At a Silver Wedding party
Peter Dainty

Thank you, God, for my birthday –
for fun and games,
for food and drink,
for birthday cake and candles,
for cards and presents,
but especially for all my friends
to share it with.
And most of all for Mum *(and/or)* Dad.
Thank you, God.

A child's birthday party
Peter Dainty

God bless (*name)* on *his/her* birthday.
Thank you that *he/she* is such an important member
of our family, and very much loved by us all.
May *he/she* enjoy this day and every day,
knowing that life is a precious birthday gift
from you.

A family meal on a birthday
Peter Dainty

Long though (*ninety*) years may seem
  they pass as quickly as a dream.
But when you've lived them one by one,
  you know they haven't really gone;
  they're all inside you, in your soul;
  your memory preserves them whole.

They're also in your mind and heart
  and in your body – every part.
Your sparkling eyes, and smiling face,
  and friendly voice, display a grace
  which didn't drop out of the blue –
  it's taken (*ninety*) years to brew.

It's taken (*ninety*) years so far
  for you to grow to what you are.
For time's the loom on which God weaves
  the tapestry of human lives.
So thank him for each precious year,
  which made your life and brought you here.

And we shall thank him too, because
  we're glad you've shared your life with us.

For a seventieth/eightieth/ninetieth birthday party
Peter Dainty

Blessed be thou, Lord God,
  who bringest forth bread from the earth
  and makest glad the hearts of thy people.

A Hebrew Prayer
for Sabbath, Passover or Harvest

For all thy gifts we bless thee, Lord,
but chiefly for our heavenly food:
thy pardoning grace, thy quickening word,
these prompt our song that God is good.

A harvest grace
John Hampden Gurney (1802–1862)

We thank thee, Lord, for this fair earth.
the glittering sky, the silver sea;
for all their beauty, all their worth,
their light and glory, come from thee.

So, while we gaze with thoughtful eye
on all the gifts thy love has given,
help us in thee to live and die,
by thee to rise from earth to heaven.

A harvest grace
George Edward Lynch Cotton (1813–1866)

Father, give us thankful hearts
to see this food upon our table.
May we remember those in need
and help as much as we are able.

A harvest grace
Peter Dainty

Thanks be to God, our Father,
for all things bright and good:
the seedtime and the harvest,
our health, our life, our food.

Accept the gifts we offer
for all thy love imparts,
and, what thou most desirest,
our humble, thankful hearts.

A harvest grace
Matthias Claudius (1740–1815)
Translated by Jane Montgomery Campbell (1817–1878)

We thank you, Lord, for times of recreation
when we can rest and play and talk and laugh,
and forget for a while our daily duties
and responsibilities.

We thank you for food we haven't had to cook,
and for dishes we don't have to wash,
and rooms we don't have to clean,
and ask your blessing upon those who work
that we might enjoy this time of relaxation.

A holiday grace
Peter Dainty

We give you thanks, O Lord our God,
for every gift your mercy sends:
for earthly beauty,
life and peace;
for faith and hope;
for food and friends.
Bless this our meal,
and give us grace
to share your gifts with joy and praise.
Amen.

For any happy gathering
Peter Dainty

For particular people

Those around the table bow their heads in silence.
A grace for Quakers and Trappists

Thank God. Amen.
The Royal Navy grace

God save the King,
  bless our dinners,
  make us thankful.
Amen.
Admiral Lord Nelson (1758–1805)

For good food,
  good friends,
  soft landings,
  we thank God.
The Parachute Regiment

God bless our food; God guard our ways,
and give us grace his name to praise
and ever keep in paths serene
Elizabeth, our gracious queen.

Composed for Queen Elizabeth I (1565)

Lord God, you know how much I need
good food to give me strength and speed.
I come to you to take my fill,
and grow in fitness, drive and skill.
So please receive this humble grace,
and give me power to run the race.

An athlete's grace
Peter Dainty

In an unjust world

We thank you, heavenly Father,
for the abundance of our harvest,
but we ask that the noise of our thanksgiving
may not drown the cries of the needy,
until we can all rejoice together
in the fullness of your kingdom.

A harvest grace
Peter Dainty

As we enjoy our meal together,
may we not turn this grace into disgrace
by our over-indulgence in a world
where many are under-nourished, for Christ's sake.

Peter Dainty

Lord, teach us how to live simply,
that others may simply live.

Christian Aid

As we feast on food
that is fit for the children of God,
let us not forget those
who can only pick up the crumbs
that fall from the rich world's table.

See Mark 7:27, 28 and Luke 16:19-21
Peter Dainty

We meet around this table
to share our daily bread,
and ask that, in your mercy,
the hungry may be fed.

Peter Dainty

Lord, as we enjoy the company of friends,
may we never forget the needs of strangers.

Peter Dainty

Lord of heaven and earth, we ask
that in our eating and drinking
we may neither damage our health
nor harm the planet,
and that all those whose labour
has brought this food to our table
may be justly rewarded,
for your kingdom's sake.
Amen.

Peter Dainty

We thank you, Father, for our daily bread.
May we never rest content
until all people can share together
at the feast of your kingdom.

Peter Dainty

Dear Father God, to you we pray:
please send the food we need today.
Remember those who may have none,
and please provide for everyone.
Anon

Lord, bless our food
and give food to the hungry.
Satisfy those who hunger
for justice and righteousness.
Peter Dainty

CHARGES

Biblical charges

Be strong and full of courage.
Do not be timid or afraid,
for wherever you go
the Lord your God is with you.
Joshua 1:9

Remember that what the Lord requires of you
is to do justice, to love mercy,
and to walk humbly with your God.
Micah 6:8

All authority in heaven and on earth has been given to me.
Go, therefore, and make disciples of all nations,
baptising them
in the name of the Father,
and of the Son, and of the Holy Spirit,
teaching them to observe
all that I have commanded you;
and lo, I am with you always to the close of the age.
Matthew 28:19, 20 (RSV)

I appeal to you therefore, brethren,
by the mercies of God,
to present your bodies as a living sacrifice,
holy and acceptable to God,
which is your spiritual worship.
Do not be conformed to this world,
but be transformed
by the renewal of your mind,
that you may prove what is the will of God,
what is good
and acceptable and perfect.

Romans 12:1, 2 (RSV)

May God the Father,
out of the wealth of his glory,
grant that you be strengthened with might,
through his Spirit in your inner being,
that, through faith,
Christ may dwell in your hearts.
So, being rooted and grounded in love,
may you be able to understand with all the saints,
what is the breadth and length and height and depth,
and know the love of Christ
which is beyond knowledge,
and be filled with all the fullness of God.

Ephesians 3:16-19

Let your love be unpretended;
hating evil, cling to good;
love with warm and kind affection
all the Christian brotherhood;
only rival one another
in the honour you impart;
never flagging in your efforts,
serve the Lord with passionate heart.
In your hopefulness rejoicing;
in adversity endure.
Let your prayers be never ceasing,
let your alms relieve the poor;
may you always give a welcome
to the stranger at your door.
Share the joy of those rejoicing,
share the tears of those who weep,
and to those who persecute you
blessings give, but curses keep.
Live in harmony with others,
never proud, but humble be,
meeting evil, not with evil,
but with true nobility;
and as far as you are able
live at peace, in deed and word,
never giving way to anger,
leaving vengeance to the Lord.
If your enemies should hunger
quench their thirst and give them food.
Be not overcome by evil;
conquer evil with great good.

Romans 12:9-21

Take up all the armour of God,
that you may be able to stand firm on the day of evil,
and when all is done, still to stand.
Stand, therefore, having girded your loins with truth,
and having put on the breastplate of righteousness,
and having shod your feet
ready to spread the gospel of peace.
Over all hold up the shield of faith,
with which you will be able to quench
all the flaming darts of the wicked one.
Also receive the helmet of salvation,
and the sword of the Spirit,
which is the word of God.

Ephesians 6:13-17

Rejoice in the Lord always;
again I say, rejoice!
Let everyone know your patience . . .
For the Lord is at hand;
therefore do not be anxious about anything,
but in everything,
by means of prayer and supplication,
with thanksgiving,
make your requests known to God.
And the peace of God,
which is beyond all understanding,
will keep your hearts and your minds
in Christ Jesus.

Philippians 4:4-7

Whatever is just, whatever is pure,
  whatever is lovely, whatever is of good report;
  if there is any excellence,
  if there is anything praiseworthy,
  fill your minds with these things.

Philippians 4:8

Put on, then, as the chosen people of God,
  holy and beloved,
  deep compassion, kindness, humility,
  gentleness and patience,
  bearing with one another,
  and, when any has a complaint against another,
  forgiving each other.
Just as Christ forgave you – you do the same.
And to all these add love, which binds together perfectly.
And let the peace of God preside in your hearts –
  the peace for which you were called into one body.
And be thankful.
Let the riches of Christ's word live in you,
  as you teach and edify one another in all wisdom
  with psalms and hymns and spiritual songs,
  singing with grace in your heart to the Lord.
And whatever you do, in word or in work,
  do everything in the name of the Lord Jesus,
  giving thanks to God the Father through him.

Colossians 3:12-17

We exhort you, brothers and sisters,
admonish the idle,
encourage the fainthearted,
help the weak,
be patient with them all.
See that none of you repays evil for evil,
but always seek to do good
to one another, and to all.
Rejoice always, pray constantly,
give thanks in all circumstances;
for this is the will of God in Christ Jesus for you.
Do not quench the Spirit.
Do not despise prophesying,
but test everything,
and keep hold of what is good.
Abstain from every kind of evil.

1 Thessalonians 5:14-22 (RSV)

I charge you in the presence of God
and of Jesus Christ, who is to judge
the living and the dead,
and by his appearing and his kingdom:
Preach the word, be urgent in season and out of season,
convince, rebuke, and exhort,
be unfailing in patience and in teaching.

2 Timothy 4:1, 2 (RSV)

Therefore, since we are surrounded
by so great a cloud of witnesses,
let us also lay aside
every weight, and sin which clings so closely,
and let us run with patience
the race that is set before us,
looking unto Jesus,
the pioneer and perfecter of our faith,
who, for the joy that was set before him,
endured the cross,
despising the shame,
and is seated at the right hand of the throne of God.

Hebrews 12:1, 2 (RSV)

Dismissals

Go forth into the world in peace;
be of good courage;
hold fast that which is good;
render to no one evil for evil.
Strengthen the faint-hearted;
support the weak;
help the afflicted;
honour all people;
love and serve the Lord,
rejoicing in the power of the Holy Spirit.
And the blessing of God Almighty,
the Father, the Son and the Holy Spirit,
be upon you, and remain with you for ever.

The 1928 Prayer Book, alt.

Go forth today in the might of heaven,
in the brightness of the sun,
in the whiteness of the snow,
in the splendour of fire,
in the speed of lightning,
in the swiftness of wind,
in the firmness of rock.
Go forth today in the strength of God.

Irish (Eighth century)

May the Lord take your minds and think through them.
May he take your lips and speak through them.
May he take your hearts and set them on fire with love.
What you know not, may he teach you.
What you have not, may he give you.
What you are not, may he make you,
for Jesus Christ's sake.
Amen.

Anon

Let us go forth
in the goodness of our merciful Father,
in the gentleness of our brother Jesus,
in the radiance of the Holy Spirit,
in the faith of the apostles,
in the joyful praise of the angels,
in the holiness of the saints,
in the courage of the martyrs.

Let us go forth
in the wisdom of our all-seeing Father,
in the patience of our all-loving Brother,
in the truth of the all-knowing Spirit,
in the learning of the apostles,
in the gracious guidance of the angels,
in the patience of the saints,
in the self-control of the martyrs.
Such is the path of all servants of Christ,
the path from death to life eternal.

Celtic

Grant, O God,
that the ears that have heard the voice of thy songs
may be closed to the voice of clamour and dispute;
that the eyes that have seen thy great love
may also behold thy blessed hope;
that the tongues which have sung thy praise
may speak the truth;
that the feet which have walked thy courts
may walk in the region of light;
that the bodies which have partaken of thy living Body
may be restored to newness of life.
Glory be to thee for thine unspeakable gift.

The Malabar Liturgy (Fifth century)

Go, labour on, spend and be spent,
thy joy to do the Father's will.
It is the way the Master went;
should not the servant tread it still?

Go, labour on, while it is day;
the world's dark night is hastening on.
Speed, speed thy work, cast sloth away;
it is not thus that souls are won.

Toil on, faint not, keep watch, and pray;
be wise, the erring soul to win.
Go forth into the world's highway;
compel the wanderer to come in.

Toil on, and in thy toil rejoice;
for toil comes rest, for exile home.
Soon shalt thou hear the Bridegroom's voice,
the midnight cry, 'Behold, I come!'

Horatius Bonar (1808–1889)

Now go in the strength of God,
to relieve the oppressed,
to hear the groans of poor prisoners,
to reform the abuses of all professions;
that many be made not poor
to make a few rich;
for Jesus Christ's sake.
Amen.

Based on a prayer by Oliver Cromwell (1599–1658)

Other charges

Christ has no body now on earth but yours,
no hands but yours, no feet but yours.
Yours are the eyes through which
he must look out with compassion on the world.
Yours are the feet with which
Christ is to go about doing good.
Yours are the hands with which
he now gives his blessing.

St Teresa of Avila (1515–1582)

Lord make us instruments of your peace:
where there is hatred let us sow love.
where there is injury, pardon,
where there is doubt, faith,
where there is despair, hope,
where there is darkness, light,
where there is sadness, joy.

O Divine Master,
grant that we may not so much seek
to be consoled, as to console;
not so much to be understood, as to understand;
not so much to be loved, as to love.
For it is in giving that we receive;
it is in pardoning that we are pardoned,
it is in dying that we awake to eternal life.

A prayer
often ascribed to St Francis of Assisi

Thanks be to thee, Lord Jesus Christ,
  for all the benefits and blessings
  which thou hast given to me,
  for all the pains and insults
  which thou hast borne for me.
O most merciful Friend, Brother and Redeemer,
  may I know thee more clearly,
  love thee more dearly,
  and follow thee more nearly,
  day by day.

St Richard of Chichester (c.1200–1253)

Fight the good fight with all thy might;
  Christ is thy strength and Christ thy right.
Lay hold on life, and it shall be
  thy joy and crown eternally.

Run the straight race through God's good grace;
  lift up thine eyes, and seek his face.
Life with its way before thee lies;
  Christ is the path and Christ the prize.

Cast care aside; upon thy guide
  lean, and his mercy will provide.
Lean, and the trusting soul shall prove
  Christ is its life, and Christ its love.

Faint not nor fear, his arm is near;
  he changes not, and thou art dear.
Only believe, and thou shalt see
  that Christ is all in all to thee.

John Samuel Bewley Monsell (1811–1875)

Teach us, good Lord,
to serve thee as thou deservest:
to give and not to count the cost,
to fight and not to heed the wounds,
to toil and not to seek for rest,
to labour and not to ask for any reward
save that of knowing that we do thy will.

St Ignatius Loyola (1491–1556)

Trust in God.
Let nothing disturb you,
let nothing frighten you.
All things pass,
but God never changes.
Patience achieves
all it strives for.
He who has God
finds he lacks nothing.
God alone suffices.

St Teresa of Avila (1515–1582)
Written on her bookmark.

Go forward through the change and chance of time
with the light of eternity in your eyes,
the inspiration of truth in your minds,
the song of the gospel in your hearts,
and the strength of well-doing in your hands.
But above all, go forward with Christ by your side:
the Way, the Truth and the Life.
Amen.

Peter Dainty

DOXOLOGIES

Biblical doxologies

Who, among all the gods, O Lord,
is anything like you?
Who is like you in majestic holiness,
in awesome splendour,
doing wonderful works?

Exodus 15:11

All people that on earth do dwell,
sing to the Lord with cheerful voice.
Him serve with mirth, his praise forth tell;
come ye before him and rejoice.

The Lord, ye know, is God indeed;
without our aid he did us make.
We are his folk, he doth us feed;
and for his sheep he doth us take.

O enter then his gates with praise;
approach with joy his courts unto.
Praise, laud, and bless his name always,
for it is seemly so to do.

For why, the Lord our God is good;
his mercy is for ever sure.
His truth at all times firmly stood,
and shall from age to age endure.

William Kethe (d.1594)
Metrical version of Psalm 100

Praise the Lord, all nations!
Worship him all, peoples!
For great and sure is his love towards us;
  and his faithfulness is everlasting.
Praise the Lord!

Psalm 117

Praise the Lord!

Praise him, all you heavenly angels.
Praise him, beings in outer space.
Praise him, galaxies and planets,
  blazing sun and moon's bright face.

Let creation praise the Lord,
  for he formed you by his word.

Praise him all you varied weathers:
  rain and sunshine, frosts and snows.
Praise him, lightning, praise him, thunder,
  praise him, every wind that blows.

Let creation praise the Lord,
  for he formed you by his word.

Praise him, all his green creation,
  plants and hedgerows, flowers, and trees;
  filling earth with wealth and beauty,
  bearing fruit your God to please.

Let creation praise the Lord,
  for he formed you by his word.

Praise him, all you living creatures
  in the sea, the earth, the sky;
  swimming, creeping, running, flying,
  praise the Lord your God on high.

Let creation praise the Lord,
  for he made you by his word.

Praise him, people of all ages,
  rich and poor and weak and strong.
Praise the Lord your God who made you;
  join together in this song:

God is great, there is none greater!
Praise his name all heaven and earth
  for he reigns through all creation,
  brings all things that are, to birth!

Inspired by Psalm 148

Praise the Lord!
Praise God in his holy place!
Praise his glory in the heavens!
Praise him for his mighty works!
Praise his all-transcendent greatness!
Praise him with the sound of trumpets!
Praise him with guitars and keyboards!
Praise him with both drums and dancing!
Praise him with the strings and woodwind!
Praise him with the loud percussion!
Praise him with harmonious voices!
Let everything that breathes adore him,
and with music praise the Lord!

Psalm 150

Holy, holy, holy is the Lord of hosts;
the whole earth is full of his glory.

Isaiah 6:3 (RSV)

Glory to God in the highest,
and on earth peace
among those who please God.

Luke 2:14

O the depth of the riches
and wisdom, and knowledge of God!
How unsearchable are his judgements
and how inscrutable his ways!
For from him, and through him, and to him
are all things.
To him be the glory for ever.
Amen.

Romans 11:33, 36 (RSV)

To him who by the power at work within us
is able to do far more abundantly
than all we ask or think,
to him be glory in the Church,
and in Christ Jesus, to all generations,
for ever and ever.
Amen.

Ephesians 3:20, 21 (RSV)

To the King of ages,
immortal, invisible,
the only God,
be honour and glory
for ever and ever.
Amen.

1 Timothy 1:17 (RSV)

Praise be to God,
the blessed and only authority,
the King of kings and the Lord of lords,
who alone has immortality
and dwells in unapproachable light;
whom no human being has ever seen,
nor can see.
To him be honour and eternal power.
Amen.

Based on 1 Timothy 6:15b, 16

Now to him who is able to keep you from falling
and to present you without blemish
before the presence of his glory with rejoicing,
to the only God, our Saviour
through Jesus Christ our Lord,
be glory, majesty, dominion, and authority,
before all time and now and for ever.
Amen.

Jude 24 (RSV)

To Jesus Christ, the faithful witness,
the first-born from the dead,
and the ruler of earthly kings;
To him who loves us
and has freed us from our sins by his blood,
and made us kings and priests
in the service of his God and Father,
to him be glory and power
for ever and ever.
Amen.

Based on Revelation 1:5, 6

Holy, holy, holy is the Lord God Almighty,
who was, and is, and is to come!

Revelation 4:8b (RSV)

Worthy are you, O Lord our God,
to receive glory and honour and power,
because you created all things,
and by your will they came to be
and were created.

Revelation 4:11

Amen! Blessing and glory
and wisdom and thanksgiving
and honour and power and might
be to our God for ever and ever!
Amen.

Revelation 7:12 (RSV)

Great and wonderful are your works,
Lord God, the Almighty!
Just and true are your ways,
O King of the nations!
Who shall not fear you, Lord,
and glorify your name?
For you alone are holy.
All nations shall come and worship you,
for your righteousness has been revealed.

Revelation 15:3, 4

Praise our God, all you his servants,
you who fear him, small and great.
Hallelujah!
For the Lord our God, the Almighty reigns.

Revelation 19:5b, 6b (RSV)

Other Doxologies

Glory be to the Father,
and to the Son,
and to the Holy Spirit,
as it was in the beginning
and ever shall be,
world without end.
Amen.

The Gloria Patria

Glory be to God on high,
and in earth peace, good will towards men.

We praise thee, we bless thee,
we worship thee, we glorify thee,
we give thanks to thee for thy great glory,
O Lord God, heavenly King,
God the Father almighty.

O Lord, the only-begotten Son, Jesus Christ:
O Lord God, Lamb of God, Son of the Father,
that takest away the sins of the world,
have mercy upon us.
Thou that takest away the sins of the world,
receive our prayer.
Thou that sittest at the right hand of God the Father,
have mercy upon us.

For thou only art holy; thou only art the Lord;
thou only, O Christ, with the Holy Ghost,
art the Most High, in the glory of God the Father.
Amen.

The Gloria in Excelsis

Praise be to the Father.
Praise be to the Son.
Praise be to the Holy Spirit.
God, the three in one.

Celtic

God, all powerful, most holy,
  sublime ruler of all,
  you alone are good –
  supremely good,
  fully, completely good.
May we render to you all praise,
  all glory, all thanksgiving,
  all honour and all blessing.
May we always ascribe to you alone
  everything that is good.
Amen.

St Francis of Assisi (1181–1226)

Hail, gladdening light, of his pure glory poured
  from the immortal Father, heavenly, blest,
  holiest of holies, Jesus Christ our Lord!

Now are we come to the sun's hour of rest;
  the lights of evening round us shine;
  we hymn the Father, Son, and Holy Spirit divine.

Worthiest art thou at all times to be sung
  with undefiled tongue, Son of our God,
  giver of life, alone;
  therefore in all the world thy glories, Lord, they own.

Anon (Third century)
Translated by John Keble (1792–1866)

O God, whose glory the heavens are telling,
the earth your power, the sea your might,
and whose greatness all the hosts of heaven proclaim;
to you belong all glory, honour, majesty and praise,
both now and for ever, and to the ages of ages.
Amen.

The Liturgy of St James (Fifth century)

All praise and thanks to God
the Father now be given,
the Son, and him who reigns
with them in highest heaven,
the one eternal God,
whom earth and heaven adore,
for thus it was, is now,
and shall be evermore.

Martin Rinkart (1586–1649)
Translated by Catherine Winkworth (1827–1878)

Praise, O praise our God and King!
Hymns of adoration sing!
For his mercies still endure,
ever faithful, ever sure.

Glory to our bounteous King!
Glory let creation sing.
Glory to the Father, Son,
and blest Spirit, Three in One.

Henry Williams Baker (1821–1877)

Praise to the living God!
All praisèd be his name,
   who was, and is, and is to be,
   for aye the same!
The One Eternal God
   ere aught that now appears:
   the first, the Last, beyond all thought
   his timeless years!

Formless, all lovely forms
   declare his loveliness.
Holy, no holiness on earth
   can his express.
Lo, he is Lord of all!
Creation speaks his praise,
   and everywhere, above, below,
   his will obeys.

His Spirit floweth free,
   high surging where it will.
In prophet's word he spake of old,
   he speaketh still.
Established is his law,
   and changeless it shall stand,
   deep writ upon the human heart,
   on sea, on land.

Eternal life hath he
   implanted in the soul.
His love shall be our strength and stay
   while ages roll.
Praise to the living God!
All praisèd be his name,
   who was, and is, and is to be,
   for aye the same.

Medieval Jewish Doxology translated by Max Landsberg (1845–1928) and Newton Mann (1836–1926)

Blessing and honour, thanksgiving and praise,
more than we can utter,
be unto you, O most adorable Trinity,
Father, Son and Holy Ghost,
by all angels, all people, all creatures,
for ever and ever, Amen and Amen.
To God the Father, who first loved us
and made us accepted in the Beloved;
To God the Son, who loved us,
and washed our sins in his own blood;
To God the Holy Ghost, who sheds the love of God
abroad in our hearts,
be all love and all glory,
from time and for eternity.

Thomas Ken (1637–1711)

O holy, holy, holy Lord,
thou God of hosts, by all adored,
earth and the heavens are full of thee,
thy light, thy power, thy majesty.

Anon
in Philip Gell's Collection of Psalms and Hymns (1815)

Glory to thee, my God, this night
for all the blessings of the light.
Keep me, O keep me, King of kings,
beneath thine own almighty wings.

Praise God, from whom all blessings flow.
Praise him all creatures here below.
Praise him above, ye heavenly host.
Praise Father, Son, and Holy Ghost.

Thomas Ken (1637–1711)

This, this is the God we adore,
our faithful, unchangeable friend,
whose love is as great as his power,
and neither knows measure nor end.

'Tis Jesus, the first and the last,
whose Spirit shall guide us safe home.
We'll praise him for all that is past,
and trust him for all that's to come.

Joseph Hart (1712–1768)

Blessed be the everlasting God,
the Father of our Lord!
Be his abounding mercy praised,
his majesty adored!

Isaac Watts (1674–1617)

May none of God's wonderful works
keep silence night or morning:
bright stars, high mountains,
the depths of the seas,
sources of rushing rivers.
May all these break into song as we sing
to Father, Son, and Holy Spirit.
May all the angels in the heavens reply:
Amen! Amen! Amen!
Power, praise, eternal glory to God
the only giver of grace.
Amen! Amen! Amen!

Egypt (Third century)

Praise the Lord! Praise the Lord!
Let the earth hear his voice!
Praise the Lord! Praise the Lord!
Let the people rejoice!
O come to the Father, through Jesus the Son;
  and give him the glory – great things he has done!

Francis Jane van Alstyne (1820–1915)

To Father, Son and Holy Ghost,
  the God whom we adore,
  be glory, as it was, is now,
  and shall be evermore.

Nahum Tate (1652–1715) and Nicholas Brady (1659–1726)

Acknowledgements

The Publishers wish to thank those who have given their permission to reproduce copyright material in this publication.

1. Page 14: The Lord bless you . . . (Hermann Shaluck), taken from *Praying in the Franciscan Spirit* by Sister Frances Teresa, published by Kevin Mayhew, 1999. © Copyright control.

2. Page 15: O God, who knowest . . . *(The Book of Common Prayer),* The Crown, Cambridge University Press.

3. Page 33: Bless this house . . . (Helen Taylor), © 1927 Boosey Co. Ltd; reproduced by permission of Boosey & Hawkes Music Publishers Ltd.

4. Page 34: The Sacred Three . . . (Alastair MacLean), taken from *Praying in the Celtic Spirit* by Frances Kelly, published by Kevin Mayhew, 1999. Used by permission of Hodder & Stoughton.

5. Page 40: I said to the man . . . (Minnie Louise Haskins). © Copyright control.

6. Pages 41-43: Three prayers from *How to be a Great Godparent* by Susan Hardwick, published by Kevin Mayhew, 2003.

7. Page 120: Go forth into the world . . . *(The Prayer Book),* © The Archbishops' Council, 1928.

Every effort has been made to trace the owners of copyright material and we hope that no copyright has been infringed. Pardon is sought and apology made if the contrary be the case, and a correction will be made in any reprint of this book.